© Marnie Christensen. All Rights Reserved.

No part of this book may be reproduced, stored in a retrieval system, or transmitted by any means without the written permission of the author.

First published October 16, 2024
ISBN: 979-8-3434871-0-7

For Andy, my real-life storyteller...

HALF A TALE

Witches aren't real.

Everybody knows that! Everybody but me. Because I know better.

"Goodnight, Jasmine," my dad said one evening.

"Wait, Dad! Can you tell me a story?"

My dad always told the best stories. He recited them from memory because that's what his dad did, and his dad's dad did. Even his dad's dad's dad! I'm almost sure.

"I would love to! But no questions this time, alright? It's getting late…"

He settled down on the edge of my bed and cleared his throat.

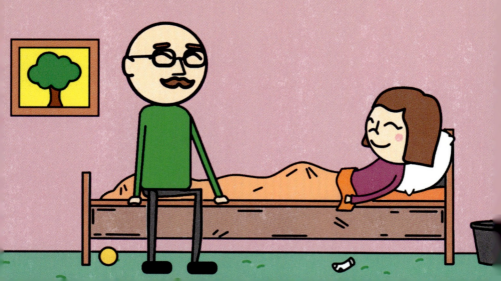

"Witches are real. Everybody knows that!

Some of them are hundreds of years old. So old, they live with other old things, like trees and turtles."

"How do they live to be so old?" I asked.

He chuckled before answering.

"Well Jazz, they steal little children's hair! They lay it in their gardens to grow the most delicious mushrooms and make mushroom soup! Their mushroom soup is said to be so scrumptious, that it tastes like sunshine, if you can imagine what sunshine tastes like."

"What kind of powers did the witches have?"

"They could cure animals! One witch, one of the oldest ones, once had a cat that she loved very much. And back when the cat was young and foolish, it would wander off to the butcher's shop. One time, the butcher found the cat stealing a chunk of chicken from the shop window. The butcher tried to catch the cat, but it was too fast! So, the butcher followed the cat home – back to the witch's cottage."

"What happened then?" I asked in awe.

"Well, the butcher realized it was the witch's cat, so decided not to catch it. But he did do something not very sensible – that means not good. He made a split-second decision, the worst type of decision you can make! He threw his butcher's carving knife at the cat."

"Was the cat alright?" I demanded to know.

"Kind of. The knife soared through the air and hit the cat's tail, cutting off the tip. The witch heard the cat cry out in pain, and came out of the house to save him."

"Was the witch mad at the butcher?"

"Oh yes. Inexplicably mad. That means so mad, you can't even explain it."

"Then what happened?" I asked, bouncing up and down on the edge of the bed next to him.

He only smiled and tousled my hair.

"I'll tell you another time."

"*What?!*" I protested. But he left my room.

No matter, I thought to myself. *I will find out what happened to the butcher.*

For I, Jasmine Twiddler, at only the tender age of eight, was a witch hunter.

2 MY HUSBAND

"Hey Tommy! Oh, I mean, hey Mrs. Reid! Is Tommy home?"

"Hi Jasmine. Yes, he's in the backyard. Would you like some soup?"

It was the summer holidays and Tommy's mom was busy in the kitchen. Tommy was my best friend in the whole world. He was actually my husband. You see, we got married during our very first recess together. I was still wearing the fuzzy, pink elastic ring he gave me all those years ago.

"No thanks, Mrs. Reid."

I walked through the house and out into the backyard where Tommy was crouching low in his fort. The fort, which Tommy had dubbed 'Backyard Biodome,' was a pile of sticks overtop of his mother's garden.

"Hey Tommy, what happened to your hair?" I said sitting down beside him.

"My mom cut it yesterday. What? You don't like it?"

"Well, yeah, it looks alright. It's kind of short though."

"Yeah, but it's not ugly, is it?"

"No, definitely not ugly! Why did she cut it so sh–"

But my eye caught something before I could finish asking my question. A small clump of hair – Tommy's hair – was lying on the ground in the garden.

"Tommy... Why is your old hair out here?"

"This is where my mom cut my hair. Why?"

"Why would she cut it out here?"

"Well, she doesn't want hair in the house. She always cuts my hair outside. Your dad doesn't do that?"

"No..."

I thought about my next question silently for a moment.

"Hey Tommy... How old is your mom?"
"We just celebrated her 38th birthday."
"That's old," I said. "Really old."
Silence again.

I'd known Tommy for two whole years. Was it possible his mom was a witch?

Then I spotted something that made my heart skip a beat. There, growing innocently in the musty garden bed between a bunch of flowers – a mushroom!

3 RECONNAISS-ANCE

It had been a week since that fateful day in Tommy's mom's garden. I had been doing my best to keep tabs on the suspected witch, following her wherever she went.

It just so happened Tommy's mom worked as a veterinarian in the shop next to the nearby corner store. Today, Tommy joined me as I sat in the corner store window, watching.

"I still don't quite get it," he said, slurping down a bright blue Gulpilee. "Why do you think my mom's a witch?"

"Shh!" I looked over my shoulder. No one was there except the store clerk who was busy picking his nose. "I told you. Your mom cuts your hair outside to feed her mushroom garden and then she makes sunshine soup with them. All witches use little kid hair of course!"

"Right, and why would she make sunshine soup?"

"To live forever!" I said with emphasis. "And to save animals, like cats that are missing half their tails."

I lifted my binoculars up again to peer at the veterinary shop. Tommy's mom was just coming out.

"This is it!" I jumped up from my chair. "Let's go!"

We left the corner store in tip-toe fashion. Tommy's mom always walked home from work with a small bag hung over her shoulder. Today, however, she was carrying a large grey bin – Mr. Bins – Tommy's faithful sidekick.

"What is Mr. Bins doing with your mom, Tommy?"

"She asked if she could borrow him this morning. He said he didn't mind so I let her."

"Quick, she's looking around – hide behind that bush!"

Mrs. Reid didn't see us, but she quickened her pace. Whatever she was carrying must have been heavy.

"Hurry – we're going to miss whatever's inside Mr. Bins!"

Within minutes, we reached the bushes outside Tommy's house. Mrs. Reid had entered the house just a moment before us and closed the door behind her.

"Let's go look through the window."

We silently edged closer to the front porch. Careful not to get pricked by the rosebushes, we peered into the house.

It was difficult to see anything at first, but then our eyes adjusted to the low lighting.

Mr. Bins was laying on the floor, empty, and Mrs. Reid was sitting on the couch, holding something black with large yellow eyes. Mrs. Reid lifted the strange creature up into the air – it was a black cat with only half a tail.

Tommy and I gasped in horror.

"Jasmine! Help me! I think my mom's a witch!"

SUNFLOWER JAM

"Ready to hear more of the story tonight, Jazz?"

"No thanks, Dad. I'm actually kind of tired."

"Oh, really? Okay."

My dad looked a little disappointed as he left my room, but I had no choice! Tonight, I had work to do.

When I was sure the coast was clear, I got out of bed and snuck down the hall.

Creeeaaaak.

I swung the door of my sister's room open. Even in the dark, I could still see the heaps of pink stuffed animals that coated the floor like a carpet. *What a princess!*

I tiptoed over the fuzzy mounds and stopped in front of the open window. On a shelf overhead was a pile of books. You see, my royal sister of noble blood loved animals of every kind – even cats! And I, knowing nothing about them, was about to get my hands on a book that would help me prove my theory – Tommy's mom had a witch's cat!

I climbed up onto the windowsill and reached towards the books. *Yes! Got it!*

At that moment, a cool nighttime breeze wafted into the room, making my sister's door slam shut with a loud bang! The princess squirmed in her bed, and I lost my footing on the windowsill.

"YIKES!"

I quickly tried to grab hold of anything in sight. But it was no good. With my hand still clutching the cat book, I fell out of the window!

"Ouuucchhh..." I groaned.

I had landed in a giant patch of sunflowers. Getting to my feet, I could see a Jasmine-shaped hole in the sunflower garden. Sunflower seeds were strewn everywhere, along with – a note! I picked it up. It was from Tommy!

It read:

I found more mushrooms.

THIS IS SPENSIBLE

Truth be told, I was only a budding witch hunter. I'd never caught a real witch before. Never even seen one. I just knew they existed. So, when I donned my battle gear the next morning, I wasn't sure what to bring with me to Tommy's house.

"Hey Dad, do you know where my slingshot is?" I called.

There was no answer.

"Princess? Where's Dad?"

Nothing.

Huh, I thought. *Guess they left already.*

In the end, I decided to wear a hairnet over my head to protect my hair and grabbed a knobbly stick to poke the witch in the eye if she got too close.

When I got to Tommy's house, I found another note pinned to the door.

Come arund the bak
-Tommy

I followed the instructions and went through the side gate to the backyard. Tommy was in his biodome as usual.

"Look," he said, pointing at a clump of mushrooms.

I looked around the garden. They were everywhere.

"This is spensible!" I said.

Tommy looked at me, confused.

"My dad says it means not good! Think about it! She's going to live forever, stealing little kid hair for centuries!"

"What about the book? Did you bring it?"

"Yes," I said. "But it's useless. Just a bunch of nonsense about how to properly care for ordinary cats. Nothing about magical ones."

"Well, now what?"

"I don't know. If she wasn't your mom, I'd say we call the police. But she is your mom. So, I guess we just make sure she doesn't steal any more hair."

But it was too late. At that moment, my dad and the Princess came out of Tommy's house.

My jaw dropped. My sister, with her pink dress and matching shoes, now had a short ponytail on the top of her head.

"How to do like your sister's haircut, Jazz? Pretty cute, huh? Mrs. Reid said she'd do yours next."

Oh no! Oh no, oh no, oh no!

THE BUTCHER'S SON

I'd managed to escape the witch earlier that day by faking a stomach-ache. Luck was on my side. But now the situation was getting dire. I needed to know the end of the tale so I could defeat the witch!

"Ready to hear the rest of the story tonight, Jazz? Why do you have a notebook?"

"Just for – you know – notes," I said.

My dad chuckled.

"Alright, here we go! Fear coursed through the butcher. He knew the witch was on to him, so he made a mad dash for his own house. When he reached it, he quickly woke his sleeping son and hauled him to the nearest inn – that's a kind of hotel. The witch wouldn't think to look for them there, the butcher thought."

"But she did! Didn't she?" I breathed.

"Yes, she did. In the morning, the butcher woke with a start. His son was yelling because he was completely -- **BALD!** The witch, it seemed, had stolen his son's hair. All of it."

I looked up at my own dad's bald head. "All of it?"

"All of it," my dad said. "And, even more shocking, the hair never grew back! The butcher's son was bald for the rest of his life. And so was his own son, and his son's son, and even his son's son's son! I'm almost sure."

"Really Dad?"

"Really," my dad said with a wink.

"Okay, but what happened next?"

"Well, nothing more happened to the butcher or his son. The witch never took anything else from them and they never saw her again. But, the cat, who had some nerve, continued to come back to the butcher's shop and steal meat. The butcher's son saw it all the time, and knew it was the same cat, because of its tail."

"Sooo... how did they defeat the witch?"

"Well, they never did of course! Like I said, they never saw her again. The lesson here is never to follow a witch's cat!"

I sighed.

"But there must be a way to defeat a witch..."

"Oh? And how would you do it?" my dad asked with a smile.

"I don't know," I admitted. "But I do know how the butcher's son could have found her."

"Oh really? How?"

"I'll tell *you* another time."

My dad laughed as he left my room. I quickly jotted down three words on my notebook so I wouldn't forget what to do next.

Follow the cat...

ONE THOUSAND MUSHROOMS

"Tommy!" I hissed. "Get behind me, quick!"

Tommy and I had put my plan to action the very next day – wait until his mom was out of the house and then let the cat lead us to – whatever it was witches hid from their victims. We were just now busy following the cat from room to room, spying on it.

"Tommy, quick, it'll see us!"

Tommy jumped from behind a flowerpot over to the sofa where I sat under a blanket.

"We need to stay still and quiet," I said. "Or else it will know we're watching it."

We waited.

Creeeaaaak.

I recognized the sound. It was the sound of a door opening.

"What's it doing?" Tommy whispered.

"I'll take a look."

I peeked out from behind the blanket. The cat was in the kitchen pantry, climbing on a shelf. A loud sound exploded from upstairs – Tommy's younger brother, Bleep, and the Princess were playing together. The sound startled the cat, and it jumped and ran out of the kitchen, knocking a book to the ground as it fled.

"Ugh!" Tommy groaned. "We'll never get this done!"

I pushed the blanket off and walked over to the book on the ground. It was a handwritten cookbook, and the page it was flipped open to had a big hand drawn picture of a mushroom on it.

"The witch's soup potion!" I screamed. "Tommy! Tommy, look at this!"

We both stuffed ourselves into the tiny pantry, closed the door, and crouched over the book. Neither of us actually dared to touch it.

"It says here to add ten mushrooms! Wonder if that means you'll live another ten years."

"Maybe if you add one thousand mushrooms, you'll live until you're one thousand!"

"Does it say anything about curing animals? Or if the soup tastes like sunshine? Then we'll know for sure."

Tommy froze.

"I think I hear someone coming!"

The pantry door handle started to turn. The door pulled open – Tommy's brother and my sister stood looking over us.

"What are you guys doing?" Bleep asked.

The Princess giggled.

"Maybe they're holding hands!"

THE SALTY STORE CLERK

I knew what I had to do. Tommy and I had figured it out and were busy saving up our allowance. Just a few more quarters and we would have enough to buy our secret ingredient.

"Hey Dad, can I wash a few more windows for you? Or organize your sock drawer?"

"Wow Jazz! You sure are working hard. What are you saving up for?"

"It's a secret. I think I figured out how to stop the witch from stealing hair. I'm sure it will work, and when it does, maybe your hair will grow back!"

My dad doubled over laughing.

"You know what, kiddo!" he said finally, wiping a tear from his eye. "You've worked hard enough. Here's a few more quarters."

"Thanks Dad!"

I ran to Tommy's house.

"Tommy! I've got enough. Let's go!"

Together, we made our way to the corner store. We grabbed the largest bag off the shelf and carried it over to the store clerk.

"Are you sure about this Jasmine?" Tommy asked.

"Yes! One time, I accidentally put some of this stuff on my cereal instead of sugar. I nearly died. This stuff is the opposite of sunshine. It will cure her for sure! Your mom will be a normal mom after this!"

The store clerk rang our item through the till. "That will be $7.99," he said.

"Uh oh. We only have $7.75! Tommy, do you have any more money in your pocket?"

Tommy shook his head.

"This is spensible," he said.

"Sorry kids. Come back when you have more money."

"But we need this! His mom's a hair-thieving witch! **It's the real-life truth!**"

The store clerk sneered. "Well, you still don't have enough money."

I planted my feet on the floor and stood up to my tallest height.

"If you don't sell us this bag right now, I'll tell everybody you pick your nose."

SOUP'S ON

"Okay, now hand me the bag!" I said.

We were in Tommy's kitchen, stirring a big pot of boiling water. Tommy hesitated, but eventually handed over the large bag from the corner store. It had one giant word written on it – *SALT*.

"Well, here goes nothing!"

I poured the bag into the boiling pot of water and stirred until I could no longer see any clumps.

"Now we just have to give her a bowl of this soup – our own special recipe – with ten cups of salt rather than ten cups of mushrooms – and she'll be cured!"

Tommy groaned.

"Relax, Tommy, your mom will be so happy not to be a witch anymore, she'll probably thank us! Right, now let's go give it to her before it gets cold."

We left the kitchen with a heaping bowl and made our way over to Mrs. Reid, who was busy petting her pet cat in the living room.

"Uh, Mom?" Tommy said. "We made you some soup."

"Oh, wow kids! That's kind of you," Mrs. Reid said, taking the bowl from me. "Mmm, smells good!"

We each held our breath, waiting.

Slowly, Mrs. Reid scooped out a large spoonful of soup and gulped it down.

At first, nothing happened. Then her eyes popped. Then her eyes shut tight. Then her head hung limp off her shoulders. Then her head snapped back. Then she made the most awful, strange collection of sounds I'd ever heard!

Mrs. Reid threw her black cat off her lap and bolted to the bathroom.

"Mom?" Tommy called as we ran after her. We came to a halt outside the bathroom door.

"Mrs. Reid? Are you okay?"

There was silence for a moment before we heard the flushing of a toilet. Then Mrs. Reid, with beads of sweat dripping off her brow, opened the bathroom door.

"WHAT ON EARTH DID YOU PUT IN THAT SOUP?"

THE GOOD WITCH

Ting! Ting!

The jingle of a door chime rang out as the front door of the veterinary shop opened.

"Ah, I thought I might find you here."

It was my dad. Tommy's mom had told him about the soup fiasco yesterday, and today he had followed me to her veterinary shop.

"Have you come to apologize to Mrs. Reid?" he asked.

"Yes, but also to see if she's still a witch," I said.

My dad smiled. He sat down on a chair next to mine.

"You know, I think I forgot to mention a little piece of that old story. Got time to hear it now?" he asked.

I looked over the counter, towards the back of the shop where I could just see Mrs. Reid checking the wings of an old, turquoise parrot.

"I have time."

"Good," he said. "I should have told you the full story. The butcher's son actually decided not to go looking for the witch."

"Really?" I asked. "Why?"

"Well... all things considered — that means he thought about all things first — the butcher's son realized the witch was using her powers for good. Helping injured animals, like the cat. I think he decided she wasn't bad after all, but actually, a good witch. And I think he thought that was worth a little bit of hair."

My dad smiled again, tousled my hair, gave me a wink, and left the shop without another word.

I watched through the window as he walked toward the corner store, then looked back over the counter towards Mrs. Reid, who was busy staring inside the parrot's mouth now.

"Polly's had too many crackers!" she said to the bird.

"Too many crackers!" the parrot squawked, horrified.

Making up my mind, I walked over to the counter and grabbed a pair of scissors off the desk.

I cut a small chunk of my hair off my head, and left it on top of a notepad, on which I wrote four simple words before leaving the shop too.

Looking for more? Check out some other fantastic reads!

The Bird, The Fish, and The Mouse are Beginner Books for ages 3 to 5. Our friend, Mouse, learns tips and tricks to spell new words. The books were inspired by my dog, Wylie, who loves chatting with little critters!

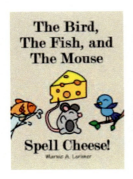  

There Was a Monkey in My Room, *There Was a Fairy in My Class*, and *The Christmas Market with Grandma* are Rhyming Books for ages 4 to 6. Rhyming Books teach phonemic awareness, fluency development, and language formation!

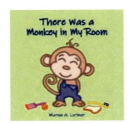  

Harold the Raindrop and *Sophia the Seed* are Science Based Books for ages 5 to 8. They teach kids about the water and plant life cycles. They were inspired by my children's elementary school teachers!

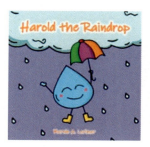 

The Real Life Truth Series are Chapter Books for ages 8 to 10. They were inspired by my budding story-tellers, who always claim their stories are "the real-life truth." I hope you live for outlandish tales like they do!

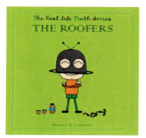 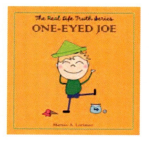

Manufactured by Amazon.ca
Bolton, ON

41499979R00024

Meet Jasmine, the witch hunter! She is convinced her friend's mom is a real witch and is stealing little kid hair to make her potions. Jasmine becomes determined to turn her back into a normal mom. Throughout this magical tale, Jasmine learns not to judge a book by its cover and teaches others that people can surprise you!

The Real Life Truth Series is a series of chapter books for ages 8 to 10. They were inspired by my budding story-tellers, Isaac, Philip, and Natalie, who loved to tell outlandish stories. When finished, they would always claim their stories were "the real-life truth." I hope you live for outlandish tales like they do!

ISBN 9798343487107